MW01487590

THE SCHOLARSHIP SYSTEM

6 Simple Steps on How to Win College Scholarships and Secure Financial Aid

By Jocelyn Paonita

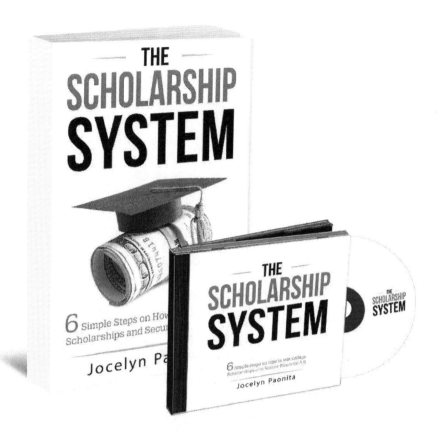

DOWNLOAD THE AUDIOBOOK AND ACTION GUIDE FREE!

I've found that readers have the most success with this book when they use the Action Guide as they read. Just to say thanks for buying the book, I'd like to give you the Audiobook & Action Guide **100% FREE!**

WWW.THESCHOLARSHIPSYSTEM.COM/ACTION-GUIDE

PAGE

TABLE OF CONTENT

1

INTRO: Breaking Down the Barriers to a Higher Education and Debt-Free Life

5

STEP 1: Getting in the Money-Making Mind-set
• Limiting beliefs
• Discovering Your Motivations
• Goal Setting the Right Way
• Accountability

17

STEP 2: Understanding College Financial Aid 101
• College Cost Calculator
• FAFSA
• Loans
• Grants
• Scholarships
• Cash Awards

27

STEP 3: The Hunt Is On: Finding Scholarships That Have Little Competition Yet Can Fund Your Free Ride
• What to look for: Navigating your way through the endless scholarships out there
• Hide & Seek: Finding scholarships where no one else is looking
• The Google Keyword Connector

37

STEP 4: Heat Up Your Application – Successful Strategies on Becoming a Competitive Candidate
• Competitive Candidate Chart
• Getting involved
• Tailoring Accomplishments to Meet Scholarship Criteria

53

STEP 5: Crushing Scholarship Applications One at a Time Choosing your process
• Finding the best scholarships for you
• Blasting through the application, one section at a time
• Packaging – making your application's appearance show how awesome you are

67

STEP 6: You've Won the Money – Closing the Deal So More Money Comes Your Way
• Thank you letters
• Receiving Your Big Bucks
• Tax Implications

71

THE SCHOLARSHIP SYSTEM RESOURCES

FOREWARD

It's now common knowledge that the total amount of student loan debt in America has topped $1.2T and the average college student will graduate with around $30,000 in loans. What isn't as well known is the fact that of the $600B worth of loans that are currently in repayment, 1 in 3 of the loans are beyond 30 days delinquent and 1 in 5 are considered in default (beyond 90 days). The other $600B is held by students either still in school or in forbearance. What we have is the very beginning of a national emergency.

What someone could deduce from these facts is that there are a growing number of students who are finding student loans rather problematic to pay back. Interest rates are higher than they've ever been, tuition has skyrocketed over the past few years, and a graduates' chances of being underemployed are just about as good as them being employed.

Thankfully, there is another way to DO college. The book you now hold in your hands is one of the greatest (and simplest) guides I have ever seen to master the scholarship process. The author is not just a researcher or someone out to make a quick buck by writing a book -- she's someone that dominated the scholarship search, application, and collection system to the tune of over $125,000.

I've been delivering a message of financial literacy on college campuses for the better part of a decade and have met student after student that received benefit from scholarships. Individually they would tell me they received the Coca-Cola Scholarship, the Gates Millennial Scholarship, lots of smaller awards or a full-ride scholarship from their school. Each had done what was necessary to obtain the award, but none could tell me in exacting detail how they went about the search, application and interview process... until Jocelyn Paonita.

The process of going after scholarships should be treated like a process, or a system as Jocelyn has so beautifully described in this book. Her notion of "the mindset" is spot on, as is the idea of goal-setting prior to getting started.

If searching for award options is what you dread most, her dead-simple process for searching google for scholarships is ridiculously good. In short, she's an expert and should be listened to.

What I've found most impressive about Jocelyn and her Scholarship System is the passion with which she wants to share it with the world. She could have been a broke college graduate with tens of thousands in debt, but instead she created a system that afforded her an amazing college experience, zero debt, and a future full of freedom and flexibility. Her goal now is to help others do the same.

Follow her advice, apply the wisdom of this book and the accompanying guide, and take charge of your financial future by graduating with as little debt as possible.

To your future,

Adam Carroll
Chief Education Officer, National Financial Educators
Author, Winning The Money Game
www.AdamSpeaks.com

BREAKING DOWN
THE BARRIERS TO A HIGHER EDUCATION
AND DEBT-FREE LIFE

Paying for college yourself has become nearly impossible. It is said that the average student acquires nearly $30,000 in debt; however, the numbers you hear more often are actually anywhere from $50,000 to $80,000 to even $150,000 and higher. When higher education is nearly the same price as a mortgage, and is increasing at a much higher rate than inflation, you have to ask whether the $40,000 salary is worth the price tag. It takes years before you get a return on your investment.

And if you are an average student in the median income level without any crazy circumstances to make you stand out for scholarships, it is especially hard for you. With all these obvious challenges, it is no wonder that students and parents feel discouraged and helpless when it comes to financial aid and paying for higher education.

But I have great news for you — it doesn't have to be such a disheartening situation. You have an alternative option that can not only shockingly reduce the debt you take on but perhaps even boost your spending money while going through college. This option is applying for scholarships and other financial aid. You don't have to pay those crazy prices in order to get a degree but you do have to go through the steps in order to make it more reasonable.

Now, this isn't an easy option if you don't know what you are doing. It can be astoundingly overwhelming with dozens of scholarship search engines, thousands of essay topics, and deadlines that range from junior year in high school to junior year in college. There are even scams out there where you fill in your information and it can be sold to other companies. I completely understand how easy it can be to just throw in the towel and give up because you feel overwhelmed or you don't meet the requirements since you are above a certain family income level, do not have a perfect GPA and you do not see yourself as the next Tim Tebow.

There are plenty of reasons why this is a tough thing to do.

That is why I have created this book.

The Scholarship System is going to be your system to make the scholarship process as simple and painless as possible. I am going to provide you with a step-by-step guide that you can actually implement in fewer hours than a part-time job yet realize the benefits for more than four years later. I've seen many of the books out there and they have some great stuff but the problem is that they are not actionable. You can't read a chapter and get a head start on the scholarship process; you just read about how awesome that person is. With this book, it is the complete opposite. Together, we are setting you up for success, not talking about my own — all you have to do is make sure you are in the money-making mind-set and carry through the steps.

I will provide you with simple solutions for applying for scholarships so that you can save time and effort while increasing your rate of return. We will discuss where you can find scholarships that barely anyone else knows about, therefore increasing your chances of winning. We will also boost your chances by covering a fast way to write killer essays that can be perfected and easily reused for other applications. And best of all, I will give you tips and tricks on how you can catch scholarship judges' attention in a good way and make sure your application doesn't get thrown in the trash.

Lastly, I will provide you with over 20 tools and resources so that, by the time you complete reading this book, you will be well on your way to getting your college experience paid for.

These skills that you are about to learn will help you regardless of your ethnicity, gender, income level or IQ. You can be completely poor or super wealthy and yet you will still be able to implement what we are covering.

As a recent college graduate, I had to deal with the same issues you are facing not long ago. I had to figure out where to look and how to apply, what the best essay writing techniques were and how to make myself a competitive candidate. There wasn't a useful guide out there for me to use so I had to struggle to figure out what worked and what didn't. It was extremely painful but I, like you, knew I did not want to be tens of thousands of dollars in debt by the time I was trying to start off my career. What fun is a salary when all of it is going to loan payments?

This is why I am writing *The Scholarship System* for you — so that you can jump right into the scholarship process rather than recreating the wheel and having to go over all the crazy hurdles of applying on your own.

With these same tactics, I managed to bring in over $125,000 in financial aid, paying my entire college bill and even giving me some extra cash each semester. I was able to focus on my higher education rather than constantly worrying about money and how much debt I was piling up.

This is what we are going to do for you together.

I have spent hundreds of hours learning as much as possible on the scholarship system so that I can equip you with what you need. It is not a long book so, as long as you stay dedicated to the system, you will see the benefits fast!

With this book, you will have multiple scholarships in the pipeline that actually apply to you. You will be able to win heaps of scholarship money because you will know how to write a killer essay in no time that knocks the judges off their feet. You will also know how to duplicate what we do so that you can keep applying these skills for years to come. Most importantly, you will have money coming your way that will enable you to go to school for a much more affordable price or for absolutely nothing at all!

The Scholarship System is short, sweet and simple so you can take the lessons out of it and implement them right away.

I promise that if you spend 40 hours a semester following this guide, you will get paid to go to school. Now, that may sound like a lot of time but it actually boils down to only 2 hours a week. **Only two hours a week** and you can save yourself years of torture being buried in debt!

Not only that but, if you actually go through all the exercises and resources in this book, you will develop a skill set that also helps you in interviews, class assignments and winning cash awards down the road.

So, before you jump in, I want to give you the single, most important piece of advice. Literally, this is the difference between those who get a free ride and those who have to take out loans to eat.

Are you ready?

Here it is....

Do not wait any longer!

START NOW!

I am serious. Starting now gives you the best shot at making college financial aid happen. If you wait and keep putting scholarship applications off, I can't promise you will get anything. The early bird gets the worm, which is insanely true in this case. Sure you can get scholarships up until your junior year in college but you still need to START NOW to be debt free. You don't even have to know which college you are going to in order to begin.

So what are you waiting for?

Let's do this!

Start making your way through the scholarship system so that you can collect your buckets of cash and blast away a future of debt.

1

GETTING IN THE
MONEY-MAKING MINDSET

GETTING IN THE MONEY-MAKING MINDSET

Have you ever set your mind to accomplish something extraordinary and then realized you just simply never pursued it? I am sure you can think of something you said you would just dominate but never followed through. For me, I have many of these unfortunately. One example would be when I wanted to play softball. After the first season, I never signed up again. I also said I was going to start developing software—that could still happen but, to this day, I just haven't put forth the time and effort to become good at it (or even remotely useful in the subject).

On the other hand, I am sure you can think of many things that you have just stormed through and completely crushed when it came to your goals. Did you say you wanted to get all A's during a semester and then come home with the report card that showed off all your hard work? Did you decide to get a job and save up $1,000? I am sure you were unbelievably proud when you saw your bank account hit four digits. For me, this was my scholarship process. I set my mind to getting my college experience paid for, to have a nice pocket full of money so that I wouldn't be drowning in debt by the end of my four years. By being completely focused on this goal and understanding why I wanted to achieve it, I was able to succeed. I was able to win an astonishing amount of scholarships that not only covered my college bill but also gave me money for my expenses.

In upcoming chapters, I will provide you with a scholarship system that is insanely simple if you can stick to it; however, the only way you will carry through and not find yourself disgruntled and ready to quit is if we get you in the right mind-set. More specifically, we have to get you in the *money-making mind-set*.

So in this chapter, we are going to focus on blasting away any doubts you have about the process and motivate you beyond belief so that you can dominate the scholarship process. Are you ready to make some money and avoid massive amounts of college debt? If so, let's continue.

<u>You can win scholarships, too!</u>

First things first, you have to be confident in yourself and realize that you are entirely capable of winning scholarships. In order to truly believe that you are capable, let's knock out some of the limiting beliefs you may have surrounding your confidence.

Limiting Belief #1: It's too late to apply for scholarships.

Let me start off by saying this is completely untrue unless you are literally about to graduate from college. Yes, that's right. It isn't too late until the fat lady sings. Well, I mean whoever is chosen to sing at college graduation. You can apply for scholarships or even cash awards which are instantly valuable as early as elementary school and as late as your senior year in college. Here is a confession: I didn't even start applying for scholarships until my senior year in high school. Now, I don't recommend this because it adds unreasonable stress which you can avoid by starting early, but I say this to show you that it is completely possible to pull off.

Every year in college, I had more and more scholarship money because I didn't just stop applying in high school like most people do. I kept applying and, as I kept applying, I got much better at it. I would knock applications out of the park in no time because I could reuse some of my best essays and I had a fresh start to build my resume when I got to college. But we will get to those tricks later. So repeat after me:

Unless I am about to graduate from COLLEGE, it is not too late to apply for scholarship money or cash awards.

Limiting Belief #2: Everyone else is already taking the good scholarships. There is nothing left for me.

I am sure you heard the statistic that billions of dollars in scholarships go unclaimed each year. I believe this is more of a myth than a fact, BUT I will say that there is certainly a large amount of money that goes unclaimed each year. Students are so focused on applying for the big scholarships such as the Coca-Cola Scholars Award or the KFC Scholarship Award that they are missing all the little ones with private institutions. In chapter 3, we will show you how to find these little unclaimed monies that certainly pack a punch because they can add up to a free ride. But first, I need you to believe that there is plenty of scholarship money out there and it is waiting for one thing: YOU!

Limiting Belief #3: I am not a superstar or genius and I don't have any insane stories to share. Why would I get scholarship money?

I wouldn't say I was an under-achiever but I can say that I was no genius with some super IQ and I was certainly no athlete. Even my grandmother will attest to that one after I accidentally threw my bat to third base during my softball game. I think the girl on third base thought I did it on purpose but I honestly was just that terrible. I was an average kid with a minimum wage job at a fast food joint; I had good grades but I didn't really start to focus on them until my senior year in high school and my involvement was mediocre until I got involved my junior year in high school. To top this all off, I hadn't had any horrific experiences in my life, I hadn't survived any life-threatening illnesses and most of my scholarships had nothing to do with my income level at all.

To summarize, everything I did is absolutely something that you can do too. Super geniuses and future Tim Tebows can get scholarships as well using this system but that does not mean you have to be one! Just realize that there is one thing in life that trumps natural talent and that is **hard work and dedication**. This is a ridiculously important line.

Repeat after me:

99 **I am confident that I can win as much scholarship money as I need. My hard work and dedication is what will win me scholarships. Without this, natural talent can only go so far.**

Reread that sentence quickly.

Excellent. Now that we have blasted away some of your doubts, let's talk about the jaw-dropping power of that hard work and dedication we just mentioned. This is the secret little trick that, honestly, anyone can use but not many people do. It is also the one piece that will differentiate you over most of your peers.

Goal Setting: Your Ticket to Cash

"If you don't know where you are going, you'll end up someplace else"
- Yogi Berra

Confidence is crucial to your success but you will build that over time as you start knocking these scholarships right out of the park. One thing you must have in order to get to that point is **hard work and dedication**. There is no way around it. You have to be driven to succeed and truly have a desire for a free ride and debt-free life after graduating. In this section, we are going to discuss your motivations and goals and how we can use those to keep you at the front of the line in the scholarship process.

Let's start off with why you even want scholarships or to go to college. You should understand your reasons for doing this process; otherwise, it will be very difficult to make it to the finish line. And no, saying that your mom or your best friend is making you do it is not a good enough reason. If that is truly how you feel, try thinking of why they are making you do this. Dig deep down into your heart and be honest with yourself. It's the only way this will be effective.

Here are directions on how to fill out the chart. This is good stuff so you don't want to miss it. Also, make sure to keep it because you will definitely want these thoughts later on!

1   **My Goal:** We are trying to understand why you would want scholarships, to go to college and to complete the scholarship system. In the next section, we will let you set up more goals which you will choose, but first we need to think of these three topics.

2   **Why do I want this?** Try to put as many reasons as possible in this box. If you run out of room, that's great! Grab a sheet of notebook paper, copy down the table and keep chugging along. The more reasons you can put in the second column, the better your chances are of winning massive amounts of college financial aid.

3   **Who can help me with this?** This is another area where the more the merrier. Try to think of anyone who has gone to college, won scholarships or can help you go through this book. It can also be someone who perhaps hasn't gone to college but they wish they did and can help keep you motivated to work hard.

4   **What if I do not accomplish this?** Be honest with yourself. How would you feel if you did not go to college? What would be the consequences if you did not get any scholarships? How would that affect you long-term? Sure, people can skip college or just take out loans but this usually means a greater challenge getting a job or tens, if not hundreds, of thousands of dollars of debt. Once again, try to write as many consequences as you can think of.

My goal	Why do I want this?	Who can help me with this?	What if I do not accomplish this?
Ex: Going to College	To get a great job after graduating so I can support myself	My aunt who attended college, graduated with high honors and got a job	If I didn't go to college, I would not feel accomplished and will have a harder time finding a job
Winning Scholarships			
Going to College			

Whenever the going gets tough, come back to this table and read what you wrote. It will remind you why you are doing all of this and hopefully give you the boost you need to complete the next essay, go volunteer or whatever it is you are having a hard time doing.

It is never fun to do things when you do not understand why you are doing them. When it comes to the scholarship process, you now know why you are doing all of this. The best part is that you also know who you can talk to when it gets really tough. Hopefully you see the value in it. Now, let's have some more fun and let you set up some goals of your own.

Goal Setting Part II

The scholarship process is a major undertaking. There will be times when you feel like you are putting forth tons of effort and not hearing anything back. It's kind of like applying to colleges. For a while, you won't hear anything; next thing you know, you have 3 different letters in the mail all in the same week. Many scholarships are on a similar schedule so this could happen but you can't let yourself become demotivated. You have to hang in there. One way to guarantee that you will keep chugging along is to have little, achievable goals set.

In the table below, set any goal you would like to achieve. It can be about building your resume with activities such as volunteering or getting a part-time job or it can be surrounding the application process, such as how many applications you want to complete in one month or how many quality reference letters you want to have by the end of your junior year in high school.

Here are a few more topics that may give you some ideas:

Examples:

Application timelines	Volunteer hours involvement in Organizations	Deadline to have proof-reader(s) chosen
Number of essays written before starting college	Run a 10k	Deadline to complete this book
Hike the Appalachian trail		Deadline for completing application research

Tips for writing goals

The challenge of goal setting is that many people leave it too vague or they never set an end point. You can see in the table below that I have a task (spending time on scholarship applications), a way to measure my progress (2 hours a week), and I have a timeline which is my light at the end of the tunnel (when I graduate high school). Now, unless all the scholarships you receive renew each year, I would suggest doing this during your four years in college so that you can make sure you continue to have enough, but let's leave it like this for now.

When you write your goals, try to structure them like the example. Here are the three characteristics of a great goal:

- It is specific and realistic.
- It is measurable.
- It has a timeline.

Another key to a successful goal, believe it or not, is telling people about it. This is helpful because they then hold you accountable. Every year I attend a conference and come back with a ton of goals. If I kept them to myself, I would easily be able to let one drop to the side. However, because I tell multiple people my goals and sometimes even ask someone to be my 'accountability partner', I feel a greater urge to actually carry through with them.

We are going to do the same for you.

In the table below, write your goal and why you want to achieve that goal as well as select someone who will not only hold you accountable to make sure you are actually completing your goals but also help you when you get stuck. Like I said earlier, there will be times when you want to quit. That is when these accountability partners are like gold. They push you and motivate you to keep going.

Last tip before letting you set your goals: create reminders. This can be a marker board with your goals written on them, or a reminder in your phone or calendar. You can even print this sheet out and tape it on your bathroom mirror. Just use something you know you will look at frequently so that you are constantly challenged to finish what you set out to do.

Okay, now it is time to set your goals. Have fun with it! If you run out of room, feel free to grab a page of notebook paper, copy down the chart and continue. Just make sure you are being realistic and try not to overwhelm yourself.

My goal	Why do I want this?	If I get stuck?
Ex. Spend an average of 2 hours/week on scholarship applications until I graduate high school	So that I can get a free ride to college and not be bogged down by debt when I graduate	My mother – she can keep track of my efforts, push me to stick to it and reward me when I do

The main reason we are setting all these goals is to help you stay dedicated to this process and maintain that desire for a free ride to school. They wouldn't send soldiers out on a mission without setting goals first, that would be a complete failure. This is the same scenario. You cannot complete the scholarship mission without having clear goals to keep you directed and motivated.

We have 2 short topics to cover and then you will hear from another student who got her entire college experience covered by scholarships. You don't want to miss this one because she gives you some of the challenges she faced as well as her major piece of advice in order to be successful in your scholarship search.

Let's quickly talk about how the people you choose in your goal charts can hold you accountable and how you can hold yourself accountable. You may think knowing that you will have a nice pay check at the end of this process is enough, but, believe me, the light at the end of the tunnel can seem pretty far away at times. This is where these tactics come into play.

You have already decided *the who* ; now let's discuss the how. How can your accountability partner or accountability 'buddy' make sure you carry out these goals?

I would suggest setting up weekly or bi-monthly meetings. These can be very short if you are both busy but just a way to check in and see how you are doing. You can meet over the phone, via Google Hangout or Skype or you can just do it in person. The method isn't as important as you're just talking about your status on these goals, otherwise you will start shuffling your feet and slowly slip on the goals.

Now how can you hold yourself accountable?

We already talked about setting reminders and having your goals in a place where you can constantly see them such as on a marker board or your bathroom mirror. One more tip is to start a Google doc or Word doc (I like Google doc because then you can also share this with your accountability buddy) and take just 3-5 minutes a day to write the following items:

- What is the date today?
- How many hours did you work on the scholarship process? (This can include volunteering, extracurricular activities, anything you do that helps make you more competitive but you need 2 hours a week on actual applications/essays.)
- What did you accomplish? (Not what you did; what did you actually accomplish?)
- What problems did you encounter?
- Do you need anything from anyone?

This should **never** take you more than 5 minutes. If it does, try limiting your responses to 5 words maximum per question. You should just add each day below the other and slowly grow the document.

14

The greatest thing about this is that you can then go back when you are receiving all that hard-earned scholarship cash and actually see the progress you made. This slowly becomes a journal of all your challenges and triumphs so you will feel amazing after reading the document.

Let's discuss what we covered.

First, the key to surviving the scholarship process is having the right mind-set. Specifically, it is about having the money-making mind-set. In order to have this mind-set, we first blasted away your doubts about the scholarship process and helped you realize that you are completely capable of getting scholarship money. Natural talent is great so if you have that, it will certainly come handy as we go on. However, what really matters is your willingness to push through this process and put forth the effort to win the big bucks. Hard work and dedication trumps natural talent any day. If you have both, you are a lethal weapon. But if you don't think you are a super genius or anything like that, do not worry. Your efforts are what matters.

You then set some goals. First, you wrote down your motivations for why you want scholarships and why you want to go to college. You then got to create some of your goals. The cherry on top is the person you chose to hold you to these goals. Having someone to push and motivate you when times get tough is extremely important. Even more important is your ability to hold yourself accountable. We covered some basic tactics that will help you do this.

I have faith in you. You can do this. No one wants to leave college in massive amounts of debt. That not only takes away from your salary you have been so excited about but it also destroys your opportunities in college and out. Don't let debt shatter your future — get in the money-making mind-set and let's get you some scholarship money.

In the next chapter, we will explain how to navigate the crazy scholarship system. You cannot begin if you do not understand what exactly you should be applying for. Chapter 2 will be focused on giving you an understandable breakdown of college financial aid. Before we get there, here is some advice from Jenn Frazee, a college student who managed to get paid to go to school.

What was your greatest challenge finding scholarships?

My greatest challenge in finding scholarships was finding ones that applied to me. There are many, many scholarships out there for high school students, but many of them have extremely specific criteria. Local (as opposed to national) scholarships give you the best odds of actually receiving them (due to fewer applicants/competition), however many of them require your parents to be a member of a certain organization, you to be of a specific heritage, or for you to have a specific intended major for college. The biggest stipulation is usually financial need, and many students believe that they do not qualify for this specific type of scholarship. If it is required that you receive federal aid or something similar, and you do not, this obviously disqualifies you, however if the 'proof of financial need' is less specific, you should always apply anyways, because you never know what the specific organization will consider. Despite all these restrictions, I was still able to apply for about 50 different scholarships, local, national, and school-specific.

If you could give one piece of advice to students who are looking for scholarships, what would it be?

Be persistent! It is easy to get discouraged and bogged down in research and in applications; however there are tons of scholarships out there that never even get given out, because no one applies! Even if you only receive 1 out of 20 scholarships that you have applied for, it will be worth the work when you save thousands of dollars on your education.
Start early, create a strategy, and apply to as many scholarships as you can! Overall, just don't give up, because that's what the majority of students do, and if you can stick it out through all the hard work, you will be rewarded.

2

UNDERSTANDING COLLEGE FINANCIAL AID 101

UNDERSTANDING COLLEGE FINANCIAL AID 101

When reading about scholarships and other forms of aid, it can be dreadful. You hear words and acronyms like grants, FAFSA, merit-based, EFC and others that may not make sense. In this chapter, I am going to explain all of these to you so that you can start the process armed with one of your greatest tools — knowledge.

To make it more interesting, we are going to choose a college, write down how much it costs and then we will run through the true cost depending on which forms of aid you use.

Let's first calculate how much your college experience will cost. If you do not know your college yet, just decide private or public school? In-state or out-of-state? Then you can take the average costs from the College Board's site. Now I don't want to scare you but you must include at least a 2-4% tuition increase for each year until you actually go to college. To calculate the increase in tuition, fill out the formula below:

(Tuition Amount x (1.025)^years until college)

Waiting three years until school with out-of-state tuition in this sample would be: $(28{,}461 \times (1.025)3) = \$30{,}649.38$

You can also use this equation: $(28{,}461 \times 1.025 \times 1.025 \times 1.025)$

Put the number you calculated in the tuition line below. If you go to college next year, leave the tuition amount as you originally found.

Next, fill out the form below. When calculating these expenses, assume only 9 months for when you are in school which means summer expenses have to be covered by a summertime job or some income source other than debt or scholarships.

For example, if you spend $40 per month on gas, type in $40 x 9 = $360.

Keep in mind, however, that if you make applying for scholarships your 'job' in high school, you can get **paid** to go to school and perhaps even have some leftover funds to help in the summer.

Also, there are ways to make these costs lower like leaving your car home your freshman year like I did.

Annual Figures	Sample University	Your University
Wages	$3,600.00	
Gifts	$0.00	
Allowance	$0.00	
Financial aid	$0.00	
TOTAL Income	$3,600.00	
Tuition	$30,649.38	
Fees	$900.00	
Books	$1,000.00	
Supplies	$400.00	
Traditional Dorm Housing	$5,988.00	
Car insurance	$720.00	
Gas	$360.00	
Car maintenance/repairs	$200.00	
Parking	$560.00	
Cell phone monthly plan	$45.00	
Entertainment	$722.00	
Personal Expenses	$350.00	
Food/household expenses	$3,021.00	
Gifts	$0.00	
Medical expenses	$130.00	
TOTAL Expenses	$45,045.38	
(Expenses - Income)	**$41,445.38**	

Now that we have a reasonable amount for how much college will cost, let's start going through the 5 financial aid terms and how they affect your cost of college. Nothing in life is free which is clear with the loans I am going to cover; however, scholarships are the closest thing to free because they just require time. Put in hard work and you will start to make waves.

Definition 1: FAFSA - the Free Application for Federal Student Aid

Many families do not fill this out because they believe their income level is too high. I have one of the biggest pieces of advice regarding the FAFSA right here: **APPLY!**

If your parents make six figures, you may not get any income-based funding but you can still get subsidized loans. I will explain what that means in just a minute but just know that subsidized loans versus one through a bank or private institution can save you tens of thousands of dollars. **No matter how much money your parents make, you should fill out the FAFSA.**

You can find details on how to apply at www.fafsa.gov but here are some key things to know about the FAFSA:

1 Apply as soon as you can. All FAFSA awards and loans are given out on a first-come first-served basis.

2 You must apply **each year**. The good thing is that, if you have siblings, your parents only have to do it once per year for all of you at once.

3 FAFSA awards can either be grants or loans but your Estimated Family Contributed, EFC, which is calculated by FAFSA, can also help you get scholarships with your university and other private companies.

4 Most people do not know this but if you do not receive the maximum amount of grant money through FAFSA, you can call your university's financial aid office and ask them to reconsider. Ultimately, the school has power over the amount within the limit. They can increase your grant if you are truly in a financial bind.

For sources of funding, let's start off with the worst case scenario: you have to borrow all funding in order to go to college. The good news is that **85% of students receive some sort of financial aid** so do not let this section scare you. It should motivate you, however, to NOT want to deal with interest. Here we go.

Definition 2: Loans

Loans are debt which will be paid back at a higher amount than you borrowed. They can be split into two categories: Subsidized loans and unsubsidized loans.

Subsidized loans are much better than unsubsidized. When I mentioned earlier that applying for the FAFSA is valuable even if you are at a higher income level, it is because of subsidized loans. In 2012, 30.8% of students with a family income of $100,000 or more received subsidized loans. Yes, we would like these percentages to be higher but the point is this: please apply for the FAFSA!

Why is this type so much better? Let's take a look using at the example estimated cost of college.

Annual Figures	Subsidized Loans	Unsubsidized Loans
Amount Borrowed	$165,781.54	$165,781.54
Interest while in college	$0.00	$20,234.72
Loan at end of college	$165,781.54	$186,016.26
Interest after college	$52,624.62	$59,075.07
Total cost of loan	$218,406.16	$245,091.33

Assumed 4.66%

As you can see, the 'Interest while in college' line for a subsidized loan is zero. Yes, your loan is building up interest over the four years but the government actually pays it for you! You will never have to pay the government back. This means that you save $20,234.72 by having a subsidized loan versus unsubsidized just in the first four years.

Then, because this extra $20,234.72 gets added to your balance for an unsubsidized loan, your interest after graduation is higher as well. In the end, the subsidized loan will save you $26,685.17 versus the unsubsidized, which is equivalent to a down payment on a house or even a brand new car in cash. This hidden cost can drown us. We need to be aware of it.

Now it is your turn. I won't ask you to deal with calculating this on your own but there are some great calculators online that you can use.

www.asa.org/repay/calculators/graduated/default.aspx
www.finaid.org/calculators/scripts/interestcap.cgi

**How much will four years at your college cost you
if you have a subsidized loan?**

What will your monthly payment be after graduation?

**How much will four years at your college cost you
if you have an unsubsidized loan?**

What will your monthly payment be after graduation?

I am sure you find these amounts to be shocking. Maybe you find these amounts are less than you expected. Either way, $200,000 is a lot of money to spend on four years regardless of expectations. The worst part is that this example is more affordable than many other schools so many of the dollar amounts other people pay are much, much higher.

Wouldn't it be so much better if you could still get the same experience, the same education, the same degree without paying anything?

I think so. Hopefully you do too because now we start the fun stuff—grants and scholarships which you do not have to pay back!

<u>Financial Aid that You Do Not Pay Back</u>

It is terrifying when you see how much college costs. Wouldn't it be nice if other people paid that bill for you? The crazy thing is that there are tons of people out there who want to! This is through the form of grants and scholarships.

Definition 3: Grants

Grants are often need-based and they do not have to be paid back. These are offered by the U.S. Department of Education and can be accessed by filling out the FAFSA.

Definition 4: Scholarships

Scholarships are accessible to anyone and also do not need to be paid back. You can lose this money if you do not maintain a certain number of classes or other criteria, but as long as you complete your degree and fill those criteria, you will never lose it or have to pay the money back.

Scholarships can be merit-based, meaning based on performance whether it be academic, athletic, artistic, etc. and need-based which are based on the student's financial situation.

How do you receive this money?

Grant money will be sent to your college and applied to your balance. With scholarships, it depends on the foundation or whoever is giving you the money. For the most part, I suggest having it sent directly to your school so that you are not tempted to cash it in. Also, you then know it is being applied to your massive bill that we calculated earlier.

IMPORTANT NOTE: Some universities actually cap how much they will hold for you so, if you hit this maximum, they will write you a check for any amount over your bill's balance and you can have any remaining scholarships sent directly to you. Either way, know that loan, grant and scholarship money is almost always sent directly to your university so you have to stay on top of them and ensure you are getting proper credit for what you have received.

Definition 5: Cash Awards

The last item I would like to cover is a cash award. The one thing that surprised me in college is that there are awards out there that are not scholarships but do not have to be paid back and are sent directly to you.

However, the reason they fit into this category is not just because they give you money but also because many are **merit-based**. You can be poor, rich or in the median-level and still be able to apply.

Some of these are a decent amount, too. I received $3,000 my senior year in college after my bills were already covered. That was okay because, like I said, it is not a scholarship. It is literally a 'cash' award, in the form of a check, to you for your leadership, community service or some other criteria you have proven yourself in.

The way to get these is to START building your competitiveness NOW and continue as soon as you get to college. You have to prove yourself for these but these are some of the best options out there.

Lessons learned

Before we move on, let's recalculate how much college would cost you if you received scholarships. That was a trick—it would cost you NOTHING if you managed to bring in enough funding!

Doesn't that sound great? A four-year degree at the college of your choice that does not cost you a penny!

Now that we have covered the basics, we are about to get into the good stuff where you will find out how to pull that off. Get excited! Can you smell the money?

In a worst case scenario, if you have to take out loans, try to take out the unsubsidized loans like I mentioned earlier because you do not pay any of the interest while you are in college. You can only get access to these if you and your parents fill out the FAFSA each year. If you have to take out a loan freshman year but get enough scholarships for the last three years, you may be able to save any excess scholarship money and pay off that loan right away rather than pushing it out and building expensive interest.

There are multiple ways to pay for college but we all like the idea of it being free. There are many different avenues to get scholarships, which we will discuss soon, but the key is to stay motivated.

So keep chapter 1 in mind where we covered your goals and accountability partners and get ready for chapter 3 where we will find the perfect scholarships for YOU so that you can start winning that money.

Now we begin to cover the reason you wanted this book in the first place: how you can get a reduced bill, a free ride or even get paid to go to school. This all depends on your level of dedication to The Scholarship System but I know you can do it. Otherwise, you would not have gotten this far in the book, especially after that painful last section of realizing how much college costs.

3

THE HUNT IS ON:
FINDING SCHOLARSHIPS THAT HAVE LITTLE COMPETITION YET CAN FUND YOUR FREE RIDE

THE HUNT IS ON:
FINDING SCHOLARSHIPS THAT HAVE LITTLE COMPETITION YET CAN FUND YOUR FREE RIDE

If you have made it to this point in the book, you are already ahead of at least half of your fellow student colleagues. Great job!

The Money-Making Mind-set - How to build motivation and drive to push through the process	✓
Financial Aid 101 - Understanding the endless terms regarding college funding	✓
The Hunt is On - Finding scholarships that have little competition but can fund your free ride	
Becoming a Competitive Candidate, One Involvement at a Time	
The Application Process - How to knock the apps out of the park and start bringing in the checks	
You've Won the Money, now What?	

As we covered, being in the right mind-set is what success really boils down to—not just in scholarships but in anything you pursue. If you can find the motivation and drive to push through whatever barriers you meet, you will be amazed at how much you can accomplish.

You are also armed with the basic knowledge so that when you are discussing financial aid with your guidance counselor or university, you will know what is going on so that you can make the decisions that are best for you, rather than signing up for years of debt bondage.

Now, let's talk about where you can find the scholarships. Remember that we want to get you funding that you **do not have to pay back**.

That includes three types: grants, scholarships and cash awards. Grants can be found via the FAFSA and this chapter is going to cover where to find scholarships and cash awards.

More specifically, we will discuss those that apply to you and have a reasonable amount of competition where your chances are much higher than one in a million.

First, we will go over what to look for in scholarships and how to scope out those scholarships that are worth your valuable time. Then we will go over where to look for and how to find scholarships that do not have the whole country applying for them at the same time.

What to look for: Navigating your way through the endless scholarships out there

When looking for scholarships, it is important to understand that any amount helps. I know it would be nice to get a $250,000 scholarship in one shot but, unfortunately, your competition thinks that as well. The nice thing is that we are going to show you how find scholarships that still can give you a free ride but are actually reasonable to apply for. If you want to apply to the Coca-Cola scholarship or the KFC scholarship, you can still apply to everything else I am going to cover applying to. However, I am going to tell you right now that the chances of winning those are really, really slim compared to many others. Nevertheless, I wish you the best of luck and say shoot for the stars.

Instead, what we are going to focus on are scholarships in odd places that have a few to zero applicants but give you a decent amount of money. These are usually $500-$5,000, but, like I said, that adds up quickly.

So please disregard the dollar amount when you are applying. Don't look at a scholarship and say "Oh, that's only $500, I want a bigger one." Instead, think of all the things that $500 can buy such as all your groceries for the semester or text books that you normally have to pay for out of pocket.

The next point I would like to make is that you should always read the criteria before putting tons of effort into a scholarship application.

If the criteria say you must be a Florida resident with a 4.0 and own a dog and you don't meet any of those, do not apply! Your application will only be thrown in the trash. We are going to look for scholarships that specifically **apply to YOU** so that you have a good chance of winning them.

QUICK TIP

Sometimes, and I mean sometimes, criteria can be stretched a bit. Now I am not saying all the criteria can be thrown out the window but here is one that I found: I applied for a scholarship that said high school students can apply. It was recurring which means if you received the scholarship, you would get the award all four years as long as you still met the academic criteria such as a a 3.5 G.P.A, at least 12 credit hours (4 classes) per semester, etc.

I was already a freshman in college and it didn't say high school students only or college students cannot apply so I gave it a shot. In the end, I received $4,000 a year and, if I wanted to stay an extra year, I would have gotten that fourth year award as well since the funding didn't begin until my sophomore year in college. If you have questions about one of the criteria, do not be shy—give them a call to clarify. It never hurts to ask but you will never get the money if you do not ask and apply. Also, you will be on their radar if you reach out to them with great questions and in a professional manner because you already displayed initiative.

"Applying for scholarships is like applying for jobs. Most of the time, your application is thrown into a huge pool of other applications just like yours and unless you have a contact within the business, you may never hear back. The advice when applying to jobs is to have a connection introduce you or pass your name along. I found the same goes for scholarships. For every scholarship I won, I had reached out to the main contact with either a question about the application/deadline/supporting materials, or had made a comment saying thank you for letting me apply, I'm looking forward to hear back. By no means am I saying that I won every time I did this, but getting my name in their mind beforehand I believe made my application stand out and helped them to pay attention when it came in."
- Mackenzie Mylod

Hide and Seek: Finding Scholarships Where No One Else is Looking

As I said earlier, you can apply for those massive scholarships that everyone knows about. There is nothing wrong with that. They are just going to be much more challenging to win versus smaller, less-noticeable scholarships. We will now cover where to look for those that have less competition and how to find the ones that directly apply to you.

Here are some of the common places you can find scholarships:

1 **Books** – There are enormous books already created that are basically a directory for scholarships. One is called The Ultimate Scholarship Book which is released each year by the College Board. This book can be scary and overwhelming because it is literally over 800 pages, but if you go through and put tabs on the pages that have scholarships that apply to you, it will feel much more manageable. This book isn't the cheapest, but if you receive one scholarship, you have already paid for that book as well as this one. You can also just go to your local library which most likely has multiple books of scholarships.

2 **Office filing cabinets** – When I was in high school, my guidance counselors had a magical drawer of scholarships that were sent to their office. Sometimes organizations and companies just send scholarship details to schools and rely on counselors to spread the word. I highly suggest going to your guidance office and asking to see any scholarships they are aware of. I think you will be surprised at how many there are.

If you are already in college, or once you get to college, you can do the same thing with two different offices. One is the financial aid office which serves all students on campus and then you should also have a counselor specifically designated to your department or major who will know of even more scholarships. Make sure you talk to both offices to find out about potential scholarships. I received over $8,000 in scholarships through our business school and I only found out about the application because I stopped by and asked.

These same offices may have some information online as well so feel free to look there first.

Aside from school offices, another office that may be useful is that of a local organization. Local, civic organizations include Rotary Clubs, Kiwanis, Optimus Club, Knights of Columbus and Lions club but are certainly not limited to those.

 Scholarship websites – One of my favorite sites when looking for scholarships was Fastweb.com. Collegeboard.com is also a great source for not just scholarship applications but more tips and tricks on applying. There are tons of search engines out there so just be careful that you do not waste your time. The good sites have thousands of scholarships on them that have competitive criteria and require essays. If you find a site that says, 'Fill out your information and you can be randomly selected for a scholarship, that site is probably not legitimate. Unfortunately, if you truly want to receive scholarships, they are going to take more work than random drawings so please do not fall for that. They are just trying to collect your information and send you spam emails.

 Google – This is my personal favorite. It seems so simple and I believe many people attempt this for at least a few minutes but not how we are about to do it. Of course, Google is just a way to find scholarships on other sites but this can be a powerful tool. Many scholarships that exist are on sites like the ones I listed above but there are also many that are only on the company's homepage. This means that, if you limit your search strictly to scholarships databases (whether in books or on scholarship sites), you can miss out on some massive cash opportunities.

In this section, we are going to fill out a worksheet that can help you come up with terms to Google in order to find scholarships that specifically pertain to you. They will be on foundation, company or organizations' sites rather than some major scholarship database.

The goal here is to develop phrases that you can search in Google. In the table below, fill in as many boxes as possible within each category.

Under 'List activities you are involved in', list everything you do whether it be something in school such as band or basketball or any other hobby such as scrapbooking, singing, public speaking, etc.

Once you form this list, you can search each of those terms with the word 'scholarship' after it. For example, you can search scrapbooking scholarships, singing scholarships, public speaking scholarships — do you see where I am going with this? The list goes on.

You can also search the same words but with 'awards' at the end: scrapbooking awards, singing awards, etc. If nothing comes up, try 'foundations' or 'organizations' and search on their sites for scholarships. Either way, this can lead to you to many scholarships that you would never have found through the other sources we talked about. These are also the best ones to dig up because, if you could not find them through the popular methods, neither could your competition which means a much higher chance of winning the big bucks.

Here is a quick story of how a current student in pharmacy school used a similar tactic to get scholarships:

"I narrowed down the traits which make me stand out and then used those keywords to search online. For instance, I am a pharmacy student, but I am also a first generation in the United States. So, I searched under 'pharmacy' and 'first generation' to increase my chances of finding fitting scholarships.

Another strategy was to predict which corporations or brands would be more likely to give out scholarships and then search it online. For instance, Tylenol is a well-established company and gives out scholarships to students in the healthcare field. I discovered this through searching on Google whether Tylenol offers a scholarship."
- Anastasiya Plagova

The Google Keyword Connector

Directions: Google the keyword you write below + the word 'scholarship' or 'cash award'. If you do not find anything, try searching your keyword + 'foundation' or 'organization'. You can then look on the organizations' sites for scholarships.

List Activities you are involved in	List organizations you are a part of	List characteristics that are unique to you	List groups that you believe would fund scholarships	List companies you love or are passionate about	List areas or subjects you believe you are strong in
Ex. Public Speaking	Ex. Ronald McDonald House	Ex. Oldest of five siblings or first-generation student	Ex. Coaches	Ex. Walmart	Ex. Leadership, community service, arts, sciences, etc

You do not have to limit yourself to this table. I found many of my scholarships by sitting on Google and trying to come up with any combination possible that could lead me to a scholarship. Be creative and see where it takes you!

5 **Social media sites** – This wasn't as common when I was applying but I will tell you that there are a ton of scholarships on social media sites, especially Twitter. You can search for any profiles with 'scholarship' in their name and find dozens, if not hundreds, that come up. It never hurts to look here so I say give it a shot!

Recap

In this chapter, we went over what you should look for when searching for scholarships as well as the main places where you can find them. Just to refresh your memory, when searching for scholarships, be sure to look for scholarships of any amount but especially the smaller ones that can add up to a free ride. These typically have less competition. Also be sure that you meet the scholarship criteria before putting all that effort into applying for it.

Places you can search include:

- Scholarship books that you can buy or check out at the library
- Offices such as your counselor's office at high school or college as well as offices of local organizations such as the Rotary Club
- Popular scholarship search engines such as Fastweb.com
- Google using our Google Keyword Connector sheet
- Social media sites such as Twitter, LinkedIn and Facebook

Action Item

Before we move on to the next chapter, please find 5 scholarships from any of our five sources and look at the applications. To make the best use of your time, make sure they are scholarships that you can actually apply for like we talked about at the beginning.

Next, write down what areas the applications ask about. For example, do they ask about your leadership experience? If so, write down 'leadership'. Do they ask about community service involvement?

If so, write down 'community service'. This will help us in the next chapter where we find ways that you can both become a competitive candidate in the future as well as tailor what you have already done in life to sell yourself immediately.

Now let's use this to make you a competitive candidate and help you start winning that scholarship money!

4

HEAT UP YOUR APPLICATION

SUCCESSFUL STRATEGIES ON
BECOMING A COMPETITIVE CANDIDATE

HEAT UP YOUR APPLICATION

SUCCESSFUL STRATEGIES ON BECOMING A COMPETITIVE CANDIDATE

In the last chapter, we discussed where you can uncover scholarships that not only fit your qualifications but also have less competition so that you have a good chance of winning them. **This is half the battle!**

In this chapter, we are going to get specific. This will lay the foundation for writing award-winning scholarship essays.

First, we are going to cover successful strategies in building your qualifications so that you can be even more competitive when applying.

I bet some of you are thinking, *But I am already a senior in high school! I don't have enough time to get new stuff on my resume!* First, I want to say that is false. You can, and should, START NOW no matter what year you are in. As I mentioned probably too many times now, you can apply until your junior year in **college**. This means that, unless you are in your senior year **in college**, it is NOT too late for you!

Secondly, I am going to show you how we can tailor what you have been doing the last couple of years to fit these competitive areas that scholarship committees are asking about. This means that, even if you are a senior in high school, this chapter will help you.

Are you ready to supercharge your application?

I will tell you now — you will be shocked at how awesome you will sound by the end of this chapter.

To start off, we have another worksheet to help you. In the one below, we are going to brainstorm new things you can begin to get involved with in order to meet the scholarships' criteria you found at the end of the last chapter.

Here is how to fill out this chart. I also have an example in the first row.

1 Competitive Area - Write the criteria topic you found on your applications (leadership, community service, etc.).

2 Current Experience - Write down anything you have done in the past that you believe fits this subject. Do not be afraid to brag here. If you have eight different experiences in which you believe you exemplified leadership skills, write them all down. If you assisted people in any genuine way without pay, put that down as community service. We will talk more about how to fill these out in the next section.

3 New Experience - Try to think of areas where you can add involvement in your key application areas. One tip here is to make sure you would actually be interested in the activity. You do not want to sign up for activities just because you want to put them in your application. This will show right through when judges are reading your essays. If you are passionate about something, this will also show and will give you much kudos in your application. Once again, we will talk more about this next.

4 Who you can talk to about beginning NOW - This should be anyone involved already. You can talk to them about what the activity is, when you would meet, how to get signed up and, most importantly, whether or not they enjoy it.

5 When you will contact them - Set yourself a strict deadline and stick to it. As you see in my hint, you want to start NOW so set your deadline for as soon as possible but still keep it realistic, otherwise you won't do it.

Now take five minutes and fill out the chart below. If you found more than three areas the scholarships are asking for, grab a sheet of paper and continue the table.

Key Competitive Area	Current experience in this area	New experience you can achieve in this area	Who you can talk to about beginning NOW	When you will contact this person by (hint: ASAP)
Ex)Leadership	Head of shift during the blood drive	Lead/start a committee in student council	President of student council	The next school day

Your chart should not be blank at this point. You should at least have the first column filled out based on what you discovered when looking up scholarship applications. It is okay if you do not have the second and third column filled out because, in this next section, we are going to go over in detail ways you can fill them out with legitimate experiences. In the end, once this is filled up, you will have the foundation you need for your scholarship essays.

Part I: Getting Involved Now

I want to begin by confronting most students' main doubt right off the bat. Many of you think, *It is too late to get involved*. By now, I am sure you can predict what I am going to say but I am going to tell you again anyway: START NOW, it is never too late.

If you are a freshman in high school, or even a junior in high school, you can begin building your competitiveness right away. You will be ahead of the game which is great!

If you are a senior in high school or if you are actually already in college, you can use this too!

It is never too late.

Why? I know this is shocking but graduating high school does not mean you are done for in the scholarship process. You can continue applying for four more years so, if you have not already built your credentials, start now. You may need loans your freshman year but, if you follow this book, you should not have to take any out by your senior year, or maybe sooner. Each year that I was in college, my scholarship balance grew and grew because I continued to apply as the years went on. You can too!

Ways to get involved <u>that count</u>

My first and most important suggestion is that you must do something you are interested in. Do not just join an organization because you want to have something for your scholarship applications, do it because you are interested in it.

Begin by joining a club that catches your eye. This is applicable for high school and college students. Most schools have organization fairs where groups can tell students about what they do. Find out when the next one is. If it has already passed, ask your counselor to see a list of all the student groups and contact either their president or advisor for more information. Organizations are always looking for more members, especially **involved members.**

If you do not see anything that interests you, start something! Ask your counselor how to begin a student organization. You will most likely need to find an advisor but this is a great experience that shows judges that you take initiative.

Perhaps you do not want to get involved in student groups. Before thinking of alternatives, I suggest giving it a shot and joining at least one because you can learn many useful skills from your interactions in these groups. However, there are always alternatives. Another way to 'get involved' that can supplement a lack of student organizations would be working on your own business. Have an idea? Start it! It does not have to make tons of money or even anything at all but, once again, this aligns with showing initiative here and you will learn an insane amount of skills. I promise.

We have covered some general suggestions but now let's get specific. Here are the areas I frequently see on applications:

Leadership

A great way to gain leadership is by joining an organization or team of some sort and taking on responsibility. You do not have to be the president right away but try to take initiative and lead something.

For example, many student councils plan school dances, pep rallies and blood drives. A great way to show you are a leader is to take a specific task that requires multiple people and head it. Do they need to organize a photographer and set up a specific area to take photos? Grab a team and take care of it. This counts! Are you part of a football team that can use some practice running through the plays? Take initiative and set up some meeting times.

I want to mention one more way you can gain leadership experience and that is a part-time job. Part-time jobs are highly respected because we all know it is tough to balance school and work. The best part? You get paid while gaining great qualifications.

When working at a part-time job, there may be situations where you have to lead your shift or make sure everyone completes their tasks before clocking out. Sometimes you have to multi-task and be resourceful because someone did not come in for their shift. These are all challenges wherein you utilize leadership skills and are completely fair game when writing your scholarship essays. So find somewhere that will hire you and hop on the experience train to success! It does not have to be a glorified job or the place where you will start your career but anything helps (and it is always nice to get paid).

In summary, anything you do that requires initiative and the ability to guide or work with others can be considered leadership, especially if you have respectfully taken the reins and completed the task as a group.
Here are some skills you gain by being a leader:

*HINT: this will help in your essays. I will also have a major list at the end of the book for you.

42

Benefits of leadership experience	
Delegation skills	Confidence
Communication skills	Responsibility
Multi-tasking	Management skills
Time management	Problem-solving skills

What other skills do you gain by leading? Take just a few minutes to fill out the chart now. We will come back to this when discussing how to write an essay.

Now that we have gone over how to get involved and build leadership experience, start filling out the third column in your chart at the beginning of the chapter if you have 'leadership' as one of your topics.

If you get stuck, ask someone else you know who is very involved. Perhaps you can bring in your accountability partner here. I am sure they will have some suggestions!

Community Service

Another area that is commonly mentioned on applications is community service. Community service is a great way to grow as a person but it is most obviously an excellent way to give back to the people and communities around you. One thing to remember is that community service is anything where you have contributed to a group without receiving pay.

43

So please do not disregard things you have done just because they were not with a major volunteer group.

What you do want to make sure of is that you enjoy what you are doing! This is where it gets fun. You can get major credit for having an impact on your community, peers or even large groups and yet you can just be doing something you love.

Here are some examples:

Do you like cooking? Cook a meal for a low-income family or for families who have sick children at the Ronald McDonald House.

Do you like playing guitar? Volunteer to play at a nursing home or for a children's hospital.

Do you enjoy making crafts? Sew blankets for a charity organization.

Do you like playing sports? Volunteer at a summer camp or Special Olympics.

I can go on forever. Just think of something you enjoy doing and creatively come up with ways you can involve that activity with helping people.

Here are some benefits you gain through community service:

Benefits of community service	
Build Relationships	Meet diverse groups of people
Communication Skills	Learn to be adaptable
Ability to motivate others	Learn to be persistent

NOTE: Many of the benefits of leadership and community service can be interchangeable.

What other skills do you gain by volunteering? Take another five minutes to fill out the chart.

Now take a few more minutes and fill out the first table in the chapter with activities you think you can do in order to build your volunteering experience if you had that as one of your scholarship criteria.

At this point, your table should be getting pretty full.

Gaining experience in these main areas certainly helps your chances of winning scholarships. You will be shocked at how applicable just these two areas can be to any essay or interview question. If there is a topic that we did not cover, just go through the same process in coming up with ways to build your credentials. Be creative in how you can meet the requirements and, as long as you can justify them and truly say you learned, were challenged, took initiative, etc., the scholarship committee will appreciate your response.

So, once again, it does not matter if you are a freshman in high school or a sophomore in college, you should get started in these areas <u>right away</u>.

The next section covers how you can tailor what you have already accomplished to fulfil these application requirements. Yes, getting involved is important but I am sure you have some other activities on your plate that are pretty awesome already. Now we are going to teach you how to sell them.

Part II: Selling What You Have Already Accomplished

We realize you are already a rock star. Let's show the committee that.
Are you already a senior in high school? Do you need activities to write on your scholarship application but you are out of time (for this year) to start getting involved? This section is perfect for you!

Believe me, I know how it feels to look at a scholarship application and say, "Oh no, what can I put here?" but you will be surprised at how easy it can be to tailor something you have already done and show how awesome you are! You may have just overlooked it because it's a day-to-day activity for you.

You are probably already very busy. Perhaps you are constantly involved in something but you just do not know how to sell it, or perhaps you have not really been too involved but you know you have done a few great things that should count.

In this section, we will explain how to uncover activities that perhaps you did not realize were worth sharing and teach you how to sell these activities so that scholarship committees give you just as much credit as those you are competing against.

Welcome to selling 101 because that is basically what you are doing—you are selling yourself. Do not be afraid to toot your own horn because this is where it is OK to do so!

Tailoring Your Accomplishments to Meet Scholarship Criteria

Let's bring out those common topics:

Leadership
Community Service
Academics

These areas all have very typical responses that most students think they must include. Many students assume leadership means they have to be president of something, community service means they have had to be involved in the blood drive or some other nationally recognized organization for years and academics means you have to have a 4.0.

Let me tell you that THESE ARE NOT THE ONLY WAYS TO ROCK THESE SECTIONS!

There are so many other ways you can sell yourself and still be a leader or a contributor to the community or someone who does well in academics or have made a special impact somehow. Essays are meant to show the skills you have learned, challenges you have overcome and the preparation you have gained for the future.

This is where we will fill out column 2 in the chart from the last section: *'Current experience in this area'* Let's Begin.

Leadership - You do not need a title to be a leader

Leadership experience does not mean you have to have a leadership position. I know that sounds like craziness but it is true. It can be anything where you led a group—even if it is only a few people.

We talked about this earlier but any time where you have taken initiative and guided a group is leadership. This includes committees, group projects, activities with your siblings and more.

Were you in charge? Did you have to accommodate others' opinions while guiding the group to a common goal? Were you facing a major challenge for the group and had to use your problem-solving skills to come up with a solution? Oh yeah—that sounds good doesn't it?

Now don't get me wrong. Judges love to see that you have held a position in one of your student organizations so that can certainly be a goal of yours but do not think that you *have* to in order to write that you have had leadership experience.

Here are some situations that would enable you to write about leadership experience:

Sports teams	Study groups	Challenging home situations
Academic teams	Volunteering activities	Working with siblings
Class projects	School activities	Babysitting

Have you been involved in anything listed above? Then I promise that you can write a great essay explaining how you have led a group, the lessons you learned and skills you gained, thus preparing you for college and future success. I promise that you can win scholarships with these activities that you have already done.

Here are ways to analyze what you have already accomplished and see if you can use it in an essay. The goal is to think of a few situations that you can reuse in your essays. We will talk more on writing later this is just to get your mind going.

- Have you been part of any team where you helped make an executive decision and moved the team forward? Did you have to motivate the group to follow your decision?

- Did you have to coordinate others in order to complete a group project or class assignment? Did you organize a group to study for a test so that you all achieved success together?

- Have you volunteered? Did you lead the group in any way? Were there challenges your group faced for which you came up with a solution?

- Do you ever help out in the school's office? The guidance office? In class? Have you learned skills that will help you in college and your career?

- Do you have any challenging home situations? Do you have a sick family member who you choose to help out a lot?

- Do your parents work a lot? Has this made you take on extra responsibility? Can you say that this taught you any valuable life lessons or prepared you for your future?

- Do you have many siblings that you help with? Do you coordinate them so that they are not running all over the place? Do you babysit and do the same thing?

If you said yes to any of the questions above, **you already have great experience that can get you scholarship money!**

I know everyone gets worried when it is senior year and they think time has run out for gaining experience for scholarship applications but you can turn many of the experiences you have had into responses on your applications.

Community Service - Yes, it counts if it was for a smaller organization or group

Now it is time to do the same for volunteer questions.

- Have you helped a grandparent or neighbor out where you did not get paid but helped them do something they were not able to do without your help?

- Did you mow the lawn for someone because they were sick or had surgery and could not do it themselves?

- Have you found stray animals and helped find them homes? Have you visited an animal shelter and helped take care of the animals in any way?

Think of things that you have done selflessly to help others. If you did not get paid, it was most likely something you could talk about in questions regarding volunteering and community service.

Academics - No, you do not have to be valedictorian to get scholarships

The last topic I want to discuss is academics. Many scholarship applications ask for your GPA, SAT and ACT scores, class ranking, etc. These are all surrounding your academic and testing experience so far.

If you have managed to pull off all A's and you got a great score on the SAT and ACT, that is great. Supplement that with some volunteering, extracurricular activities and/or a part-time job and you are golden.

For those of you who perhaps struggled through your freshman year and have not been able to pull up your GPA, you can still earn scholarship money as well!

Yes, you heard me right. If you are not a straight-A student or have less than a 4.0 GPA, you can still receive financial aid. It will not be as easy as if you were a straight-A student but it is still possible.

How? Well let me tell you.

Many scholarship applications leave room for an 'anything else you want the committee to know' essay. Please never leave this blank! This is your opportunity to wrap up your entire application and really sell yourself. This is also where you can justify your lower-than-4.0 GPA.

Justifying less-than-perfect grades or test scores

If you have terrible grades, low standardized test scores and you do not do anything but play video games, I cannot help you. However, if you have average grades and test scores, you especially need to be involved or have a part-time job. The only justifications for lower grades are perhaps special challenges you have faced and/or extra involvement outside of the classroom that takes time away from studying. Now I am not saying you should write every excuse in the book but you can certainly explain why the scores are not where you want them to be and how you are trying to correct this. You cannot just simply admit that they are less than average and that is just where they are going to stay. You have to show that you have taken initiative to increase them and will continue to do so.

If you explain that you have lower scores and haven't studied as much as you would have liked, you should have a reason for that as well as a remedy. For example, explain (if it is true) that it is due to a part-time job and involvement with some volunteer group, however, you have recently designated a specific number of hours towards homework and studying only so that you can bring up your grades and test scores. Or you can explain that you have taken on especially challenging courses where you knew you would not get an A but decided to take the more challenging route so that you are truly prepared for college.

There are many ways to spin a less-than-perfect GPA or test score. Just be careful that you do not sound like you are just making excuses and genuinely come up with a way to remedy it.

Recap

In this chapter, I covered ways to gain experience, get involved and build your credentials so that you can knock scholarship essays and applications out of the park.

I also covered strategies to explain what you have already experienced so that you can still write an amazing essay even if you have run out of time to gain more involvement. This is especially useful for you seniors who are about to graduate.

Lastly, I covered academics and how being a straight-A student is wonderful but if you are not a straight-A student, you can justify this and still be a competitive scholarship applicant.

If you narrowed all this down to one main point, I showed how nearly every student can earn scholarship money. You just have to know how to build yourself in areas where you may need more experience and know how to sell what you have already done so far.

Now there is no excuse for not receiving scholarship money so let's start applying!

Before you move on, please make sure that you have filled in all the tables in the chapter. This will be especially helpful when writing your essays so make sure to come up with as many strategies, experiences and benefits as possible.

In the next chapter, we are going to cover a basic system for applying for scholarships and then how to write a killer essay in minimal time that can be reused to win scholarship after scholarship.

5

CRUSH SCHOLARSHIP APPLICATIONS ONE AT A TIME

CRUSH SCHOLARSHIP APPLICATIONS ONE AT A TIME

The Money-Making Mind-set - How to build motivation and drive to push through the process	✓
Financial Aid 101 - Understanding the endless terms regarding college funding	✓
The Hunt is On - Finding scholarships that have little competition but can fund your free ride	✓
Becoming a Competitive Candidate, One Involvement at a Time	✓
The Application Process - How to knock the apps out of the park and start bringing in the checks	
You've Won the Money, now What?	

In the last chapter, we discussed how to get involved as well as how to show that you are a competitive candidate with things you have already done. In this chapter, we are actually going to take that and cover how to apply for the scholarships with your new-found (or maybe it was already there) competitiveness. This chapter will be broken down into four sections:

1. Choosing Your Process – Guaranteeing success through an organized routine
2. Finding the best scholarships for YOU
3. Blasting through the application, one section at a time
4. Packaging – Making your application's appearance show how awesome you are

This chapter is extremely important. It wraps up everything we have covered and puts it into actionable items so that you can deliver a finished application that is ready to win.

Choosing Your Process – Guaranteeing success through an organized routine

The one guaranteed error students often make that will ensure tons of debt is <u>not applying</u>. But what stops students from applying? There are many reasons, I am sure; however, the main reason is that they miss the deadlines or did not manage to pull everything together correctly. So how can you avoid this to make sure you are winning scholarships? One major step forward is by simply creating a set process to prevent you from falling into these issues.

Here are some suggestions regarding your scholarship process although there are certainly different ways depending on your personality and preferred work environment.

Keep all documents, recommendation letters, resume versions, essays, etc. in one safe place.

You can certainly go the traditional way and use actual folders, but today you can also do this in a cloud-based storage site such as DropBox or Google Drive. The benefit of this is that you can access your information anywhere. Do <u>not</u> just leave your files on your computer because, if it crashes, you will lose everything. Believe me — I am speaking from experience here.

Create clearly defined folders so that you know where to find everything. Also, never delete anything. If you are creating a new version, save it as "Name _ V2" then "Name_V3", so on and so forth so that you can always back track if you need to.

I kept everything throughout my scholarship process and can still use some of the essays to this day. You never know when you will need them so make sure to keep it all organized.

2

Create calendar reminders for deadlines.
Many people now use the calendars on their phones or in their email but just remember to set some sort of reminder so that you do not miss the deadlines. Whatever your strategy is for school, use the same one for scholarship applications. Deadlines vary from summertime to fall to spring so be sure to keep that information available!

3

Utilize your accountability partners in your process.
Try to set scheduled meetings, even if they are only 5-15 minutes long. Accountability buddies are very useful and are excellent at ensuring you carry through and do not miss deadlines. Be sure to involve them in your entire process.

4

Set up a separate email account strictly for scholarship applications.
This keeps your applications and login information all in one place and keeps your personal email from being flooded with scholarship emails. Additionally, having an email dedicated to the scholarship process keeps your focus strictly on scholarships rather than other emails you are receiving.

5

Set aside a specific time that you will always use strictly for applying for financial aid.
Some people like to do their research and applying on a Saturday, others like to do it in the morning during the week. Whatever you prefer, try to set a consistent time frame where you will focus on the scholarship process. As I mentioned earlier, 40 hours a semester will be perfect for your process so try to factor that number into your timing. Either way, you want to make sure you actually carry through with the process.

Finding the Best Scholarships for YOU

Two chapters ago, you found five different scholarships for which you met the specific criteria. If you didn't, I suggest pausing now and going back to that chapter to do so. If you still do not feel like you found anything, visit worksheet _____ which will further help you in finding possible scholarship opportunities.

We have already covered this topic but here are the main characteristics you want included in the scholarships you are applying for:

1. Legitimate source: Make sure this is not just a random drawing or scam to collect your information.

2. Reasonable criteria for you: Do not waste time on applications that have requirements you cannot fill.

3. Deadline has not passed: I know this is obvious, but still, I just wanted to point out that scholarships close when they say they will close. If you really want to apply to this scholarship, set a reminder for about 8-10 months after the closed deadline so that you can apply next year. Remember—the scholarship process is not just a one-time thing, it is on-going until you graduate college so you can certainly apply next time.

4. Any dollar amount: Remember that small dollar amounts quickly add up. Those $500-$1,000 scholarships have less competition because other students think these are not worth applying for. Any amount helps so do not ignore a scholarship based on dollar amount.

Blasting Through the Application, One Section at a Time

There are five main areas of scholarship applications. The requirements certainly vary but this should cover at least 80% of what you will see.

1. General information section

This is where the scholarship committee gathers:

1. Contact information

2. University you plan to attend (this is just to get an idea so do not be afraid to list one you haven't accepted yet)

3. Cost estimate of planned university—you can use the table from Chapter 2 because you want to make sure to include all costs, not just tuition.

4. Scholarships received already

5. Planned major (once again, this is okay to change after the fact unless it is part of the requirements)

6. Current classes you are taking
7. Family history such as number of siblings, salary information and parent information

8. FAFSA information such as your Estimated Family Contribution (EFC)

This section should not take too much effort but the one point I would like to make is that you should always make sure everything is filled out, spelled correctly and is as accurate as possible. Applications can be thrown away without the essays even being read if the basic information section is filled out incorrectly.

You may have noticed that cost of your university and any scholarships already received are listed. The scholarship committees want to weigh in your need depending on the price of your higher education. It would be helpful to just keep this information in a spread sheet or Word document so that you have it available for your applications in the future.

2. Involvement

Many scholarship applications ask you to list any organizations or extra-curricular activities you are involved in, whether they are athletic, religious, academic, etc. It is helpful to keep another Word document with this information because you will have to share this more often than not.

When filling out this section, please do not forget our most recent chapter about selling what you have already done. You will be amazed at what you can list here. Do not think that you have to be president or treasurer in order to list your involvement. If you made a serious contribution, you can and should list it. If you are not sure what to put here, go back to the last chapter and reread it.

TIP: As you get involved, keep one file with the name of the organization, the date you got involved and then any leadership or volunteer experiences within it. You should also keep track of any awards you have received such as honor roll, leadership recognitions, etc. I learned this the hard way but it is easy to forget everything you have done over the last few years!

3. Essays

Now here is where you can make or break your scholarship application. I explained earlier that you do not have to be president of your organizations, you do not need a 4.0 G.P.A., but one thing you do need is a killer essay that sells what you have accomplished.

This section is going to go into detail because I want you to succeed and, if we can get a few good essays that you can reuse for your applications, you will be at least 80% where you need to be in order to get funding!

Before we go into my suggestions, here is what another recent graduate had to say about writing essays:

"Writing an essay takes a lot of time but once you finish it you can usually just make small tweaks and use it for various applications. I would say I probably wrote about 10 over the years that I used on many different occasions. One essay normally took about 3-4 hours from start to end, and I would have one of my professors look it over to be sure it was good. For big scholarships that someone at my school had won in the past, I would ask the person who had won to look it over and compare it to the one they had written."
- Mackenzie Mylod

Basic essay requirements

Before we get started on what to write, let's cover how to write your essays.

Most essays have a word or character requirement. In school, word requirements ensure you do not write too little; with scholarships, they are typically used so that you do not write too much. Do not, and I repeat, please do not exceed essay word requirements. If it says 250 words maximum, utilize the full 250 words but **do not exceed** 250. Your application can actually be thrown out if you do not follow the essay requirements.

The next point I would like to make is that you have to make sure your essays are **grammatically correct.** The biggest tip I can offer here is to always have at least one other person check it for you. When I applied for scholarships, I had multiple teachers and professors help me throughout the process but there was one teacher who consistently went through every single one of my essays. There will inevitably be errors, even with auto-correct in Microsoft Word, so please get an extra pair of eyes to take a look.

Who can review your essays? I highly suggest reaching out to a teacher or professor. Not only are they experienced in writing essays but it is also a great opportunity to get to know them better. You can also have family members and your accountability partners look at them. Either way, you want at least one other highly-experienced person to read over them.

Lastly, try to format your essays nicely. Some scholarships will just have you paste your essay into an online form but keeping your essays double-spaced, size 12 font and Times New Roman while in Microsoft Word or any other tool you use will keep them very clean in case you do need to print and mail them. Also, this makes it easier on the people reviewing your essays. Just remember: appearance is important in this case!

Brainstorming for an Essay

Remember back in elementary school when a teacher taught you how to do 'spider webs' of ideas to help you form your essay? I am not sure about you, but I know I never actually listened to them — until now. The brainstorming 'spider web' that was taught to us years ago is actually called mind-mapping and helped me write this entire book. It actually works!

When you sit down to write an essay and start writing in sentences in a document, you are writing and therefore thinking linearly. However, if you use the mind-mapping approach, you force your mind to be more creative, therefore forming a more effective essay. If you want to write an award-winning essay, you have to be creative.

Here is how to mind-map:

In the center of a blank sheet of paper, write the topic that you need to write about. For example, say the essay question is: Name a time that you had to overcome a difficult challenge. How did you overcome it? In the center of the paper, you can write challenges and then circle that word.

Then, stemming off that first word, simply keep writing any words or phrases that come to mind regarding the topic. Scatter these words all over the sheet of paper and connect them on what the idea stemmed from. If you find a piece of your mind map that you want to run with, feel free to start a new sheet of paper with that specific idea in the middle.

Once you have a full sheet of random thoughts, try to form an outline from them. Group the words or phrases into three main ideas and write this down as your outline. After you complete a quick outline, you are ready to start writing. It is amazing how quickly you can write a phenomenal essay using this method.

Selling Yourself in an Essay

Now that you have the ideas and an outline, let's talk about how to sell yourself in an essay.

The beginning of your essay should always grab the judges' attention. I always liked to start off with a quote or a story of some sort. When mind-mapping, I am sure some of your thoughts related to a story somehow. That would be a perfect way to begin. Either way, you never want to just start by rephrasing the essay question. That is very bland and probably half of your competitors are doing that. You want to start off with something that is mind-boggling or thought-provoking.

Here are a few examples:

Essay question: In your opinion, what is the greatest challenge that your generation will face? What ideas do you have for dealing with this issue?

Sample response:

"As the years go on, every individual is becoming more and more independent as well as self-sufficient – especially women. While this is an advantage, I am afraid my generation will forget that together we must make a whole - whether it consists of all United States citizens, employees for a single company, or even members of one household. Individuals can only go so far on their own and, in order to truly succeed, everyone needs to work together for a brighter future. That said, I believe the greatest challenge my generation will face involves unification as a country, community or even family."

You can see here that I used an intriguing sentence that makes the judge question "where is she going with this?" yet wrap it up at the end of the introduction so that I clearly state my answer to the question. This is much better than just saying "The greatest challenge that our generation will face is being part of a group..." Not so attention-grabbing.

One more example:

Essay question: What is one of your personal goals?

"Education is the key to success. The first to attend college within my family, I am determined to succeed with anything I embark on- especially with my career. My parents support me fully in my education but are unable to assist financially; therefore, I must find other monetary assistance. The scholarship I have received so far is one that I have worked hard to earn; however, I still do not have enough money to cover my tuition costs. Nevertheless, with my education, I plan to meet one of my personal goals and that is to make my family proud by completing college and making a difference in our country."

Hopefully you see what I mean after those examples. Now the next step is the body of the essay.

You want to keep the body very structured. As I said earlier, try to form your thoughts into three main ideas. This will help you keep the essay organized and easy to follow. In addition to keeping it organized, try to keep them interested throughout the entire essay. There are many _____ out there that help demonstrate how awesome you are. To make it even easier on you, I put a huge list at the back. These are the same words that are typically used in resumes because they are power words that catch anyone's attention. For example, of the two sentences below, which sounds better?

1. When I was part of the ACE club, I helped start a fundraiser that raised $1,000 for a charity.
2. **Establishing** a <u>successful</u> fundraiser with my team in the ACE Club, we **achieved our goal** of raising $1,000 for a charity.

The second sentence sounds much more impressive. Those key words like 'establish' and 'achieve' are great buzz words. Try to spice up what you are saying with buzz words like these because not only do they catch attention, they also articulate what you are trying to say in a better way.

Lastly, do not undersell yourself. Overall, your goal is to show that experiences throughout your life make you qualified for the scholarship award. Earlier in the book we discussed many different scenarios that can be used in essays as selling points such as helping a neighbor, volunteering with a small organization, leading a shift at work, etc. Keep in mind that all of these are challenging experiences and therefore valid responses. If the essay asks you about a challenge, do not say, "Well, I have had a pretty easy life," because that does not do anything for you. You must develop something of substance that sells you.

Let's recap:

1. Start off with an interesting story, quote or phrase that catches the reader's attention.
2. Structure the essay around three main points so that it is organized and easy to follow.
3. Include popular buzz words to sell yourself.
4. Do not undersell yourself. Remember: you need the money too!

4. Miscellaneous Scholarship Requirements

My goal is to prepare you so there are no surprises when you apply for scholarships. Here are the last few items that many scholarships ask for. Once again, not all will, but at least you are prepared.

FAFSA results – They will ask about your Estimated Family Contribution in some scholarship applications so make sure you complete your FAFSA as we discussed at the beginning of the book.

Transcripts – Many times you have to order official transcripts through your guidance office but sometimes you can send in a printout from your school instead. If the scholarship accepts a printed copy for the application, they will often ask for an official transcript later if you are selected as a recipient.

SAT/ACT scores – Some scholarships simply ask for your scores and do not require any official documentation. Others may require your official scores from the College Board.

The SAT and ACT both allow you to send your scores for free to a certain number of recipients if you write them down at registration but it will cost you a small amount after that. If you have free or reduced lunch in school, you can get waivers for a lot of this so ask your counselor if that is available to you.

Résumé – Few scholarships actually ask for a résumé but I always suggest submitting or sending one if you can. Having a solid resume as a high school student can be impressive as long as you have it properly done. I submitted a résumé with almost all of my applications because it gives them additional information that you may not have been able to fit in the application. One point to keep in mind, however, is this is very similar to an essay and you should make sure does it not have any spelling errors, does use the power words, etc. It is not worth sending if it does not sell you!

5. The 'Anything Else?' Essay

Many scholarships give you space to share any other information you feel is important. You should **always** take advantage of this opportunity. Remember when we talked about less-than-perfect test scores or grades? This is your chance to explain that. Did you really want to share your amazing experience leading a team to success in school? Here you go! Whatever you think will put the cherry on top of your application needs to be in this essay so, once again, please do not skip this!

If you are completely stuck on what to write here, try to do your 'mission statement'. In the resources section, you will find a worksheet titled 'My Mission Maker' that will walk you through some questions to brainstorm what a general essay about you can look like. Give it a shot!

I could go on forever with suggestions for writing your essays but this foundation is what you need to write some killer, award-winning essays. Just keep in mind that it takes practice. Working with the person who is reviewing your scholarship essays over and over again will only improve your writing skills and make your applications stronger each time. So do not just write a few essays and say, "Geeze, I did not win anything," instead, keep writing them and improving them constantly and, with that, keep applying. The more applications you submit, the higher your chances are of winning!

Packaging – Making your Application's Appearance Show How Awesome You Are

Remember the saying "Do not judge a book by its cover"? Unfortunately, this does not apply in the scholarship process. Judges will judge your application by its appearance. Why? Let's just think: If one judge gets two applications, both are of the same quality and have decent essays but one was nicely formatted, printed on clean sheets of paper, stapled together in the order the application requested and the other is just a ton of loose leaf sheets of paper in no order with grammatical errors, which one do you think they will select? The orderly one!

So how can you make sure your application is not thrown away for silly reasons?

First, I highly suggest putting your essays and all other requirements in the order they were listed on the application. Secondly, and I know I already said this but it is worth repeating, ensure there are no spelling or other grammatical errors anywhere. Lastly, put all of these in one nice, neat envelope for delivery.

If you are submitting online which many scholarships have moved to, your life is simpler; however, please make sure all sections are filled out correctly and, if you can, format your essays nicely after pasting them such as putting spaces between paragraphs and indenting paragraphs.

Recap

I suggest scanning through this chapter each time you are about to submit an application to make sure you did not forget anything. Also, do not forget about all the resources at the back of the book as well as on the internet. The more time you spend up front finding the right scholarships and working on your essays and perfecting them, the less time you will spend down the road because you will be able to reuse them just like I did.

Between the research skills you have developed and the writing suggestions we covered, you are a scholarship guru right now. In the final chapter, we are going to cover basic logistics of how to handle your newly found cash!

6

YOU'VE WON THE MONEY
CLOSING THE DEAL SO MORE MONEY
COMES YOUR WAY

YOU'VE WON THE MONEY
CLOSING THE DEAL SO MORE MONEY
COMES YOUR WAY

In this book, we have covered a lot of material. If you have made it to this point, you are a scholarship applying machine ready to win some money for college. I honestly am so excited for you!

We covered the basic financial aid 101 so that you understand all the different options you have. We then calculated how much school will cost you if you take out a loan which was not too pretty, I am sure. Hopefully that gave you some serious motivation to complete this book, however, we also went over getting in the money-making mind-set which is one of the most important steps in The Scholarship System because if you do not feel motivated to go through this process, you will not see the results you want.

After getting you in the mind-set with some goal setting, we then covered where to find scholarships and cash awards. You already found five scholarships that specifically match your characteristics so that you do not waste any time on scholarships that do not pertain to you.

Next, we went through a ton of different worksheets to help you find your competitive qualities and discover how you can sell them. Once we figured out what you can talk about on your applications, we covered how to apply including the basic requirements of applications, how to write a killer essay in no time that you can reuse and all the miscellaneous requirements you may see. The last step we covered was how to package your application so that it is presentable, professional and award-winning.

Now that is a lot of information!

BUT – we are not finished yet.

Let's talk about handling this money so that you keep bringing in more each year.

Receiving Your Big Bucks

Once you receive scholarship money (yes, I am that confident in you!), you will most likely have to send in your school's information so that they can send the money to the university. If your university caps you and you meet that amount, you can request the check to be sent directly to you. I do not suggest doing this until your entire bill is paid for! Otherwise, you risk spending it on non-necessity items. If your bill does not use up all the funding, the university will actually cut you a check for the remaining amount. It is beautiful, I promise.

Thank You Letters

Someone put this money towards a scholarship so that they can help students like you; therefore, it is a nice gesture to thank them when you get it. It does not have to be anything incredible but a simple thank you card can go a long way.

In the resources section, I created an outline for a solid thank you note. I suggest getting blank thank you cards or hand-writing a letter. If your handwriting is truly illegible, you can type the thank you letter but it will not seem nearly as personal as you writing it yourself. Another opportunity to thank them is when you graduate. No matter the occasion, let them know what you majored in, your future plans and how their scholarship helped you get there. It is so rewarding to hear you made an impact on someone else's life. Let them hear it!

Tax Implications

When I received my scholarship money, I was worried that I would have to pay taxes on it. By my senior year, I had thousands of dollars that were over my university bill so I was especially worried. I have good news for you—you do not have to pay taxes on your scholarship money as long as it is proven to be used for college bills. Now I am no accountant and laws change all the time but here are the basic rules I learned to play by:

Scholarships are tax free when used for:
1. Tuition and fees to enrol in an accredited institution
2. Fees, books, supplies and equipment required for your courses

Scholarship money is taxable when used for:
1. Room and board
2. Travel
3. Research

You will receive a tax sheet each year from your university regardless of whether or not it is taxable. If you had an excess amount over your college bill, you (the student) have to report this in your taxes for the past year. This did not impact my parents in any way. For more information, I suggest looking on the IRS website.

Conclusion

Anastasiya put the scholarship process into words perfectly:

"Searching for scholarships could be very rewarding, but it could also be very time consuming. Plan to dedicate several hours a week to this. The more scholarships you apply to, the higher are your chances of receiving the financial aid you're searching for."

There is a lot that this process entails but I am completely confident that you can do it. Otherwise, you would not have made it to the end of the book. I hope you enjoyed *The Scholarship System* and all the tools and worksheets we went through. I am so excited for you to start winning your scholarship award money right away.

Remember: do not stop once you graduate high school! If you can master this process and continue doing it until your senior year in college, you can make more and more money each year. Perhaps you can even get enough to pay off any loan balances from the first year if need be. Just keep applying to as many scholarships as possible as long as you truly meet the criteria.

I wish you the best of luck! Now go make some money!

For more tips and tricks, sign up at www.thescholarshipsystem.com

THE SCHOLARSHIP SYSTEM RESOURCES

● **CALENDAR**

Check out our suggested calendar from Junior year in high school all the way until Senior Year in college! www.thescholarshipsystem.com

● **ACCOUNTABILITY PARTNER LIST**

Accountability Partners			
Name	**Goal to Help With**	**Meeting Frequency**	**Method for Meeting**
Ex. John Smith	Completing 5 scholarship applications by winter break	Every Wednesday at 8:00PM	Google Hangout or Skype

● PASSWORD PROTECTOR

It is very easy to lose passwords whether they are for sites to find scholarships or even sites where you are applying. Use this table to keep track of all the usernames and passwords you need. This should keep you from having to search everywhere for your information every time you start your research or applications.

Password Keeper		
Site	Username	Password

● SCHOLARSHIP TRACKER

Scholarship 1
Site:

Login Info:

Due date:

Scholarship 1 Requestments

Scholarship 2
Site:

Login Info:

Due date:

Scholarship 2 Requestments

Scholarship 3

Site:

Login Info:

Due date:

Scholarship 3 Requestments

_____
_____
_____
_____
_____

Scholarship 4

Site:

Login Info:

Due date:

Scholarship 4 Requestments

_____
_____
_____
_____
_____

Scholarship 5

Site:

Login Info:

Due date:

Scholarship 5 Requestments

_____
_____
_____
_____
_____

Scholarship 6

Site:

Login Info:

Due date:

Scholarship 6 Requestments

_____
_____
_____
_____
_____

Six scholarship applications are not enough to get a free ride. Make copies of the Scholarship Tracker sheets and keep applying!

● PERSONAL STATEMENT WORKSHEET

COMING SOON!
Sign up at www.thescholarshipsystem.com to receive via email!

● THANK YOU NOTE OUTLINE

Dear _____,
I wanted to thank you for the __(scholarship name here)__ scholarship. Without it, I would not be able to __(what would happen if you didn't receive funding?)__. I am now majoring in __(major here)__ which I plan to use as a (profession you plan to go into). I also am getting involved in (organizations, clubs, activities you have joined).

Overall, my college experience is (adjective here such as great, amazing, life-changing) and you are part of the reason I am here. So once again, thank you for (contributing/creating/donating) to the (scholarship name here) scholarship. You have helped me get one step closer to my future success.

Best regards,

(Your name & contact information)

Power Words for Essays

Able	Earned	Managed	Recommended
Accomplished	Educated	Marketed	Redesigned
Achievement	Encourage	Maximized	Reengineered
Action	Enhance	Mediated	Represented
Advanced	Enhanced	Mentored	Restructured
Analysis	Established	Modernized	Retained
Analyzed	Evaluate	Motivated	Revised
Assist	Evaluated	Negotiated	Revitalized
Audited	Examined	Nourished	Safeguarded
Built	Facilitate	Observed	Secured
Closed	Facilitated	Obtained	Selected
Collaborated	Forecasted	Operated	Spearheaded
Committed	Formulate	Organized	Specified
Conduct	Fulfilled	Originated	Standardized
Conducted	Gained	Overhauled	Strengthened
Consult	Gathered	Oversaw	Structured
Contributed	Gave	Participated	Suggested
Coordinated	Generated	Performed	Superseded
Counseled	Headed	Pioneered	Supervised
Defined	Hosted	Planned	Targeted
Delegated	Identified	Prepared	Taught
Deliver	Impacted	Presented	Tested
Delivered	Implemented	Processed	Trained
Demonstrated	Improved	Promoted	Transcended
Design	Improvised	Prospected	Tutored
Develop	Increased	Provided	Unified
Developed	Influenced	Published	Upgraded
Devoted	Justified	Pursued	Utilized
Distinguished	Launched	Quantified	Validated
Diversified	Lobbied	Ranked	Valued
Drove	Maintained	Received	Wrote

● MIND-MAP EXAMPLE

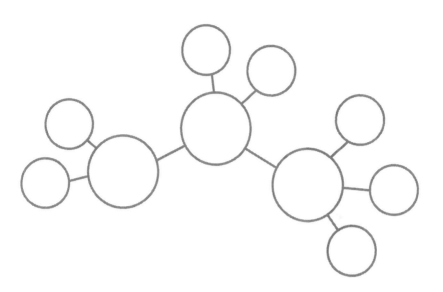

● ADDITIONAL HELPFUL SITES

www.mint.com	Budgeting, Financial Planning
Google Timer	Use timer to ensure full-time commitment to your search
Stay Focused Chrome Extension	Block distracting sites when working on scholarships
www.dropbox.com	Create folders for each scholarship and access files from anywhere
Online calendar	Set reminders for scholarship due dates and goal deadlines

45889011R00047

Made in the USA
Lexington, KY
14 October 2015